Math Mammoth

Skills Review Workbook

Answer Key

By Maria Miller

Contents

Chapter 1: Addition and Subtraction

Skills Review 1, p. 7

1.

5	8	11	14	17	20	23	26	29	32
35	38	41	44	47	50	53	56	59	62
65	68	71	74	77	80	83	86	89	92

2.

13 - 9 = blue
27 + 5 = yellow
32 - 4 = pink
14 + 9 = gray
50 - 6 = orange
48 + 7 = red
16 - 8 = green
25 + 6 = brown

3. a. $25 - 7 = ?$
   Solution: $? = 18$ are still in the box.
   b. $\$7 + \$15 + \$23 = ?$
   Solution: $? = \$45$ was how much she had originally.

Skills Review 2, p. 8

1. a. 18   b. 114   c. 42   d. 270

2.

22	−	6	=	16
+				
70	−	9	=	61
=		+		−
92		15		7
		=		=
30	+	24	=	54

3. a. 272   b. 169   c. 514   d. 345

4. $100 - 53 = ?$ or $53 + ? = 100$

5. $154 - 60 = ?$ or $60 + ? = 154$

Skills Review 3, p. 9

1. a. 24th; twenty-fourth   b. 3rd; third   c. 42nd; forty-second   d. 71st; seventy-first

2. *430*, *480*, 530, 580, 630, 680, 730

3. *210* $- 2 = 208$ $225 - 8 = 217$
   215 $- 4 = 211$ $230 - 10 = 220$
   220 $- 6 = 214$ $235 - 12 = 223$

4. a.

	4	2
2	1	9
+ 1	2	6
3	8	7

b.

		8
5	3	7
+	1	3
5	5	8

c.

2	0	5
	3	4
+ 1	1	2
3	5	1

5. a. 794   b. 547   c. 988

Skills Review 4, p. 10

1. a. 649   b. 301   c. 923   d. 714

2.

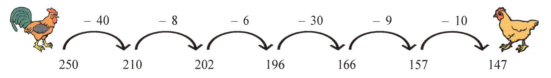

3. a. CLIII   b. LXXIX   c. LVI   d. CCCXLV   e. XVIII   f. CXXIV

4. a. 395 = 395   b. 684 < 783   c. 918 < 930   d. 72 > 71

5. a. Jasmine sold 15 more tickets than Brad sold.
   b. The three children sold a total of 43 tickets.

Skills Review 5, p. 11

1. a. 536   b. 296   c. 271   d. 340

2. a. 41   b. 17   c. 39

3. 15, 17, 19, 21, 23, 25, 27, 29, 31, 33, 35

4. 9 + _?_ = 435 or 435 − 9 = _?_   ? = 426

5. 137 − 60 + 95 + 60 = 232; The children had a total of 232 total points.

Skills Review 6, p. 12

1. **Ice Cream Cones Sold**

chocolate

vanilla

strawberry

2.   a   n   b   s   y   r   a   t   o   e   w   p
Circle the fourth letter from the right = o
Circle the twelfth letter from the left = p
Circle the eighth letter from the right = y
Circle the second letter from the left = n

What word can you make with these letters? pony

3. a. 153   b. 407   c. 760

4. a. 245   b. 283

Skills Review 7, p. 13

1. XIV = 14   CXXIV = 124
   XXXVIII = 38   XCIII = 93
   CCLIII = 253   XLVII = 47

2. a. 24 − ? = 16; ? = 8 cows were left
   b. 35 + ? = 59; ? = 24 cookies were baked by Jenna

4.

432	437	442	447	452
457	462	467	472	477
482	487	492	497	502

Puzzle corner:

 = 8 and = 6

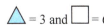 = 3 and = 6

Skills Review 8, p. 14

1. a. 237; 397 + 237 = 634   b. 574; 238 + 574 = 812

2. a. 402   b. 588   c. 749

3. a. △ = 18   b. △ = 6   c. △ = 9

4. a. 125 + 125 = 250 round trip and 109 + 109 = 218 round trip; So the total for both was 250 + 218 = 468 miles.
   b. 15 + 17 = 32 so each boy got 16 fish. Each boy had 8 fish left after they shared with Mrs. Hill.

Skills Review 9, p. 15

1. a. Mr. Williams is 12th in line from the right.
   b. Mr. Anderson is 4th in line from the right.

2. a. 466   b. 254

3. a. 92   b. 93   c. 110

Skills Review 10, p. 16

1. a. 653   b. 376   c. 996   d. 346

2. a. 33   b. 34   c. 38   d. 45

3. a. 20 > 19   b. 34 = 34   c. 50 < 70   d. 70 > 64

4. a. He still had 34 goats to catch.
   b. Initially, she had 238 stickers.

Skills Review 11, p. 17

1. a. 372; 372 + 328 = 700   b. 438; 438 + 467 = 905

2. 480 + 30 = 510, 510 + 30 = 540,
   540 + 30 = 570, 570 + 30 = 600,
   600 + 30 = 630

3. a. $49 + ? = $62, ? = $13   b. 33 − 14 = ?, ? = 19 carrots left.

4.

a. a kite, $28, and camera, $42	b. shoes, $59, and a game, $33	c. a fan, $64, and a book, $25
kite about $30 camera about $40 together about $70	shoes about $60 game about $30 together about $90	fan about $60 book about $30 together about $90

Skills Review 12, p. 18

1. a. 13th; thirteenth   b. 22nd; twenty-second
   c. 51st; fifty-first   d. 90th; ninetieth

2.

```
      4  8
   4  1  3
         5
+  1  5  1
   6  1  7
```

3.

```
220 −  5 = 215
220 − 10 = 210
220 − 15 = 205
220 − 20 = 200
220 − 25 = 195
220 − 30 = 190
```

4. a. 30   b. 70   c. 100   d. 40

Puzzle corner:

```
  7  2  1      9  8  3      8  6  8      9  3  5
−  2  6  7   −  3  3  5   −  4  7  6   −  3  7  2
  4  5  4      6  4  8      3  9  2      5  6  3
```

Skills Review 13, p. 19

1. a. 448   b. 369   c. 238   d. 216

2. a. XXIV   XXV   XXVI
   b. XLIX   L   LI
   c. XCIX   C   CI
   d. LXVII   LXVIII   LXIX

4. a. 29 + ? = 45   45 − ? = 29; ? = 16 min.
   b. 15 + ? = 72   72 − ? = 15; ? = 57 years

5. a. 250, 254, 260; 250
   b. 860, 867, 870; 870
   c. 300, 306, 310; 310

6.

231	226	221	216	211	206	201	196	191	186
181	176	171	166	161	156	151	146	141	136

8

1. It is eighteen miles.

2. It is about forty miles.

3. a. 45   b. 551   c. 440

4. a. table about $370, chair about $130, total cost about $500
   b. a skateboard about $60, sun glasses about $30, total cost about $90

5. a. He still has 253 sheep.   b. They have a total of 94 students.

Chapter 2: Multiplication Concept

Skills Review 15, p. 21

1. The flowers for Rhoda are not correct. There should be two-and-a-half flowers to represent 15.
   The flowers for Stephanie are correct.
   The flowers for Karen are not correct. There should be one-and-a-half flowers to represent 9.

2. $223 - 20 + 9 = 212$ passengers originally.

3. a. $8 - 7 = 1$; 7   b. $640 - 50 = 590$; 530

4. a. There are six sea horses between the fourth and the eleventh.
   b. There are five sea horses between the second and the eighth.

5. a. 9   b. 45   c. 197

Skills Review 16, p. 22

1. a. Tyler found the most seashells.
   b. Sandra found six more seashells than Alicia did.
   c. $14 + 19 = 33$ Jacob and Kelvin found a total of 33 seashells.

2. a. 675   b. 990   c. 860   d. 788

3. a. XXI   b. LXXIII   c. CCLXXX   d. XVIII   e. LXX   f. CXLI

4. a. $382 - 7$	b. $574 - 9$	c. $763 - 6$
$382 - \underline{2} - 5$	$574 - 4 - 5$	$763 - 3 - 3$
$= 375$	$= 565$	$= 757$

Skills Review 17, p. 23

1. a. a painting about $440 and a flute about $570; total cost about $1,010
   b. a calendar about $20 and curtains about $70; total cost about $90

2. a. $720 + 150 = 870$; $870 - 720 = 150$; $870 - 150 = 720$
   b. $91 + 36 = 127$; $127 - 91 = 36$; $127 - 36 = 91$

3. a. $17 - 9 = ?$; $? = 8$ b. $\$78 + ? = \$90$; $? = \$12$

4. Please check the student's drawings.

  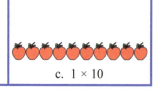

a. 3×5 b. 2×7 c. 1×10

Skills Review 18, p. 24

1. a. $12 - (4 + 6) = 2$ b. $17 - 3 - (5 - 2) = 11$ c. $(23 - 9) + 6 - 2 = 18$

2. $19 + 19 = 38$ miles round trip

3. $25 - 16 = 9$ miles further

4. 27; $27 + 678 = 705$

5. $350 + 60 = 410$; $410 + 60 = 470$; $470 + 60 = 530$

6. a. $3 + 3 + 3 = 9$; $3 \times 3 = 9$ b. $2 + 2 + 2 + 2 = 8$; $4 \times 2 = 8$

Skills Review 19, p. 25

1. a. 11th eleventh   b. 43rd forty-third   c. 61st sixty-first   d. 72nd seventy-second

2. a. $4 \times 6 = 24$

 b. $3 \times 3 = 9$

3. $22 + 18 + 22 - 7 = 55$ crickets total

4. a. Sweet Treat Bakery used 28 pounds of apples.

 b.

Apples Used to Make Pies	
Toothy's Bakery	🍎🍎🍎🍎🍎
Choo Choo Bakery	🍎🍎🍎🍎
Hungry Hat Bakery	🍎🍎🍎🍎🍎🍎
Sweet Treat Bakery	🍎🍎🍎🍎🍎🍎🍎

🍎 = 4 pounds of apples

Skills Review 20, p. 26

1. a. 942   b. 233   c. 661   d. 459

2. a. $4 + 4 + 4 = 12; 3 \times 4 = 12$ b. $5 + 5 + 5 + 5 = 20; 4 \times 5 = 20$

3. a. 54   b. 170   c. 114   d. 98   e. 93   f. 49   g. 47   h. 260

4. a. 113   b. 70   c. 725

5.

397	394	391	388	385
382	379	376	373	370

Skills Review 21, p. 27

1. a. The multiplication 4×5 is done first, then you add $12 = 32$.
   b. Multiply 2×7 and 3×3. Then you subtract 9 from $14 = 5$.
   c. Multiply 2×4 first. Then subtract 5 from $10 = 5 + 8 = 13$.

2. About $160 +$ about $230 = 390$ marbles altogether.

3. a. 430   b. 330   c. 110   d. 640

4. a. 50 fingers   b. 14 legs   c. 16 tires

5. $60 + 48 = \underline{\ ?\ }$; $\underline{\ ?\ } - 48 = 60$

6. a. $40 + 50 = 90$ and $8 + 3 = 11; 90 + 10 + 1 = 101$
   b. $20 + 30 = 50$ and $6 + 7 = 13; 50 + 10 + 3 = 63$

Skills Review 22, p. 28

1.

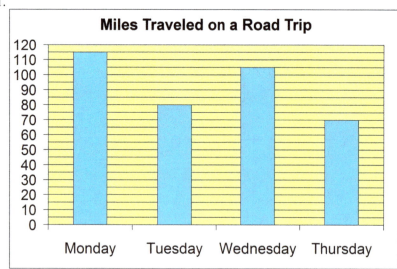

2. a. 20   b. 18   c. 10   d. 14

3. a. $3 \times 5 + 7 = 22$ rabbits   b. $3 \times 6 - 9 = 9$ pens left   c. $\$72 - 2 \times \$7 - \$27 = \$31$

Skills Review 23, p. 29

1. a. About $50 + 50 = 100$ miles round trip.

2. $9 + 27 + 24 = 60$ total miles.

3. a. 620,   500   b. 90,   50
   c. 210,   730   d. 40,   80

4. Please check the student's answer.
   Answers will vary.
   For example: A teacher bought ice cream cones
   for four girls, four boys and four teachers.
   How many ice cream cones did she buy?

Puzzle corner:

	5	6	9		6	4	3
+	1	7	6	−	3	4	4
	7	4	5		2	9	9

Skills Review 24, p. 30

1.

XXXX XXXX XXXX XXXX XXXX XXXX XXXX	XXXXXXX XXXXXXX XXXXXXX XXXXXXX
a. $7 \times 4 = 28$ seven groups of 4	$4 \times 7 = 28$ four groups of 7
XXXXXXXX XXXXXXXX XXXXXXXX	XXX XXX XXX XXX XXX XXX XXX XXX
b. $3 \times 8 = 24$ three groups of 8	$8 \times 3 = 24$ eight groups of 3

2. a. 4×3 is done first; $16 - 12 = 4$
   b. $(3 - 2)$ is done first; $5 \times 1 + 3 = 8$
   c. $(3 + 3)$ should be done first; $12 + 2 \times 6 = 24$

3. a. There are 10 doves still in the tree.
   b. She had $5 \times 5 + 58 = 83$ shells originally.
   c. The storm knocked down 39 trees.

Chapter 3: Multiplication Tables

Skills Review 25, p. 31

1.

2. a. 4 × 3 is done first; 41   b. (2 + 7) is done first; 18   c. (11 − 3) is done first; 22

3. a. 218   b. 493   c. 226   d. 624

4. a. 4 × 5 + 3 = 23 ounces of corn   b. 7 × 23 = 161 ounces of corn

5. 362 − (120 + 82) = 160 are black

Skills Review 26, p. 32

1. a. Herd 2 has eighteen more elephants than herd 3 has.
   b. Herd 4 has 36 elephants.
   c. Herds 1 and 4 have a total of 54 elephants.

2. a. 6 + 6 + 6 + 6 + 6 = 30   b. 3 + 3 + 3 + 3 + 3 + 3 + 3 + 3 = 24

3. $72 − $58 = $14 difference in price.

4.

1st	2nd	3rd	4th	5th	6th	7th	8th	9th	10th

   a. There are 4 people between the 4th and 9th person.
   b. There are 3 people between the 2nd and the 6th person.

5. a. 0   b. 8   c. 0   d. 9

Skills Review 27, p. 33

1.

7 × 2 = 14	6 × 2 = 12	3 × 2 = 6	4 × 2 = 8	5 × 2 = 10
9 × 2 = 18	8 × 2 = 16	11 × 2 = 22	10 × 2 = 20	12 × 2 = 24

2. a. 4   b. 10   c. 18   d. 22

3. a. Double 9:
     9 + 9 = 18; 2 × 9 = 18   b. Double 14:
     14 + 14 = 28; 2 × 14 = 28   c. Double 16:
     16 + 16 = 32; 2 × 16 = 32

4. a. XLIV + LVI = C   b. CLX − XXXIIII = CXXVI   c. LXII − XV = XLVII

5. a. 373 − 7
     373 − 3 − 4 = 366   b. 115 − 8
     115 − 5 − 3 = 107   c. 612 − 5
     612 − 2 − 3 = 607

6. 3 × 5 = 5

Skills Review 28, p. 34

1. a. 328   b. 214   c. 684   d. 517   e. 811

2.

a. Add 25.	b. Add 30.
_130_	_185_
_155_	_215_
180	245
205	275
230	305

3. Please check the student's answers,
   they will vary. Example: How many
   tires do three cars and nine bicycles have?

   $3 \times 4 + 9 \times 2 = 30$ tires

4. a.

$3 \times 4 = 12$	$4 \times 4 = 16$
$8 \times 4 = 32$	$11 \times 4 = 44$
$6 \times 4 = 24$	$1 \times 4 = 4$
$12 \times 4 = 48$	$10 \times 4 = 40$
$9 \times 4 = 36$	$5 \times 4 = 20$
$2 \times 4 = 8$	$7 \times 4 = 28$

b.

$6 \times 2 = 12$	$3 \times 2 = 6$
$10 \times 2 = 20$	$1 \times 2 = 2$
$4 \times 2 = 8$	$11 \times 2 = 22$
$12 \times 2 = 24$	$8 \times 2 = 16$
$2 \times 2 = 4$	$5 \times 2 = 10$
$7 \times 2 = 14$	$9 \times 2 = 18$

5. $(7+2) \times 2 \times 2 = 36$ individual shoes

Skills Review 29, p. 35

1.

a.	b.	c.	d.
$10 \times 9 = 90$	$10 \times 8 = 80$	$6 \times 10 = 60$	$3 \times 10 = 30$
$7 \times 10 = 70$	$4 \times 10 = 40$	$10 \times 2 = 20$	$10 \times 0 = 0$
$5 \times 10 = 50$	$10 \times 10 = 100$	$11 \times 10 = 110$	$12 \times 10 = 120$

2. $3 \times \$5 + \$35 = \$50$

3. a. $10 \times \$7 + \$7 = \$77$, together they have $77.
   b. $\$70 - \$12 = \$58$

4. a. 48, 28   b. 369, 399   c. 298, 338

Puzzle corner:		
$6 - 3 \times 2 = 0$	$9 \times 3 - 3 = 24$	$8 + 4 \times 7 - 6 = 30$

Skills Review 30, p. 36

1.

$7 \times 5 = 35$	$4 \times 5 = 20$	$11 \times 5 = 55$	$8 \times 5 = 40$	$6 \times 5 = 30$
$1 \times 5 = 5$	$9 \times 5 = 45$	$5 \times 5 = 25$	$10 \times 5 = 50$	$3 \times 5 = 15$

2. a. 50   b. 610   c. 50   d. 760

3.

$5 \times 1 - 2 = 3$
$5 \times 2 - 4 = 6$
$5 \times 3 - 6 = 9$
$5 \times 4 - 8 = 12$
$5 \times 5 - 10 = 15$

4. a. $4 \times 3 + 5 \times 6 = 42$ markers   b. $3 \times \$10 - \$15 = \$15$

Puzzle corner: $5 \times 7 = 35 + 2 \times 5 = 45$; She had $7 + 2 = 9$ piles of sticks originally.

14

Skills Review 31, p. 37

1. It is about 340 miles round trip.

2. 195 – 167 = 28; Adam drove 28 more miles.

3. a.

7 × 3 = 21	12 × 3 = 36
11 × 3 = 33	9 × 3 = 27
2 × 3 = 6	5 × 3 = 15
6 × 3 = 18	3 × 3 = 9
10 × 3 = 30	8 × 3 = 24
4 × 3 = 12	1 × 3 = 3

b.

1 × 4 = 4	6 × 4 = 24
7 × 4 = 28	2 × 4 = 8
11 × 4 = 44	8 × 4 = 32
3 × 4 = 12	12 × 4 = 48
9 × 4 = 36	4 × 4 = 16
5 × 4 = 20	10 × 4 = 40

4. 8 × 10 + 4 = 84 cookies.

Skills Review 32, p. 38

1. a. Mia drives 2 × 33 - 66 miles round trip. Forrest drives 2 × 26 = 52 miles round trip to work.
   b. (39 + 39) × 3 = 234 miles Bruce drives round trip in three days.

2. a. 283 + 32 = 315; 315 – 283 = 32   b. 45 + 47 = 92; 92 – 45 = 47

3.

a.	b.	c.	d.
2 × 6 = 12	5 × 6 = 30	1 × 6 = 6	12 × 6 = 72
7 × 6 = 42	4 × 6 = 24	6 × 6 = 36	8 × 6 = 48
10 × 6 = 60	9 × 6 = 54	11 × 6 = 66	3 × 6 = 18

4.

a.	b.	c.	d.
4 × 3 = 12	3 × 3 = 9	1 × 3 = 3	12 × 3 = 36
6 × 3 = 18	11 × 3 = 33	5 × 3 = 15	10 × 3 = 30
8 × 3 = 24	2 × 3 = 6	9 × 3 = 27	7 × 3 = 21

Skills Review 33, p. 39

1. a. 25 + 25 + 25 + 25 = 100 walnuts originally. or 4 × 25 = 100. There were about 100 walnuts in the 2 packages.
   b. Answers will vary. For example: Four people each ate three pieces of pizza.
      How many slices of pizza was there? 4 × 3 = 12
   c. 14 + 229 = 243 lemons.

2.

12 × 11 = 132
6 × 11 = 66
11 × 11 = 121
8 × 11 = 88
3 × 11 = 33
7 × 11 = 77

3.

a. 4 × 11	>	7 × 6		b. 5 × 7	>	3 × 11
c. 12 × 5	<	8 × 11		d. 2 × 11	>	3 × 7
e. 11 × 5	>	9 × 6		f. 9 × 11	<	10 × 10
g. 7 × 10	>	6 × 11		h. 9 × 9	>	7 × 11

Mystery number: Possible answers are: 27 or 60

15

Skills Review 34, p. 40

1. a. 5, 0   b. 0, 9   c. 10, 0   d. 7, 0

2. a. ? − 23 = 9;   ? = 32   or   23 + 9 = ?;   ? = 32
   b. 53 − ? = 47;   ? = 6   or   47 + ? = 53;   ? = 6

3. 0, 9, 18, 27, 36, 45, 54, 63, 72, 81, 90, 99, 108

4.

a.	b.	c.	d.
$2 \times 9 = 18$	$5 \times 9 = 45$	$12 \times 9 = 108$	$6 \times 9 = 54$
$7 \times 9 = 63$	$3 \times 9 = 27$	$8 \times 9 = 72$	$9 \times 9 = 81$
$11 \times 9 = 99$	$10 \times 9 = 90$	$4 \times 9 = 36$	$1 \times 9 = 9$

5. $4 \times 9 = 36$; each friend got 4 stuffed animals

Skills Review 35, p. 41

1.

a.	b.	c.	d.
$7 \times 9 = 63$	$7 \times 12 = 84$	$7 \times 7 = 49$	$7 \times 2 = 14$
$7 \times 4 = 28$	$7 \times 8 = 56$	$7 \times 5 = 35$	$7 \times 11 = 77$
$7 \times 1 = 7$	$7 \times 3 = 21$	$7 \times 10 = 70$	$7 \times 6 = 42$

2. a. 431   b. 766   c. 804   d. 687

3. a. $3 \times 4 = 12$ Each got 4 crackers.
   b. $6 \times 3 = 18$ They have 18 wheels altogether.

4. Green arrow jumps: $7 \times 3 = 21$;   Orange arrow jumps: $3 \times 7 = 21$

5. a. XXIII, XXIV   b. XV, XVI
   c. LVIII, LIX   d. CIV, CVII

Chapter 4: Telling Time

Skills Review 36, p. 42

1.
a.

$5 \times 8 = 40$	$8 \times 8 = 64$
$12 \times 8 = 96$	$11 \times 8 = 88$
$3 \times 8 = 24$	$7 \times 8 = 56$
$1 \times 8 = 8$	$4 \times 8 = 32$
$9 \times 8 = 72$	$10 \times 8 = 80$
$6 \times 8 = 48$	$2 \times 8 = 16$

b.

$4 \times 7 = 28$	$1 \times 7 = 7$
$10 \times 7 = 70$	$9 \times 7 = 63$
$7 \times 7 = 49$	$12 \times 7 = 84$
$3 \times 7 = 21$	$2 \times 7 = 14$
$8 \times 7 = 56$	$11 \times 7 = 77$
$5 \times 7 = 35$	$6 \times 7 = 42$

2. a. $9 + 15 = 24$
   b. $8 \times 8 - 28 = 36$

3. a. 73rd; seventy-third   b. 5th; fifth   c. 51st; fifty-first   d. 22nd; twenty-second

4. a. 23   b. 395   c. 101

5. $9 \times 8 + 6 = 78$ worksheets she needs to print.

Skills Review 37, p. 43

1.

a.	b.	c.	d.
$4 \times 12 = 48$	$5 \times 12 = 60$	$6 \times 12 = 72$	$8 \times 12 = 96$
$7 \times 12 = 84$	$11 \times 12 = 132$	$9 \times 12 = 108$	$12 \times 12 = 144$
$10 \times 12 = 120$	$2 \times 12 = 24$	$1 \times 12 = 12$	$3 \times 12 = 36$

2. a. 157   b. 447   c. 95   d. 415

3. a. 60 inches   b. 5 ft; 96 inches   c. 9 ft; 144 inches

4. 144, 132, 120, 108, 96, 84, 72, 60, 48, 36, 24, 12, 0

5. a. $\underline{?} - 34 = 27$ and $27 + 34 = \underline{?}$
   b. $61 - 23 = \underline{?}$ and $23 + \underline{?} = 61$ or $\underline{?} + 23 = 61$

Skills Review 38, p. 44

1. a. 624   b. 538   c. 412

2. 3:00; 2:55

3. Answers will vary. For example:
   Five children each picked eight pieces of fruit and put them in bags.
   The total weight of the bags was twenty pounds.
   Two of the children each gave away two pounds of fruit.
   How much do the bags weigh now? $20 - 2 \times 2 = 16$ pounds.

4. a. mirror about $50 + vase about $20 = about $70 total
   b. fishing rod about $120 + tent about $470 = about $590

Skills Review 39, p. 45

1.

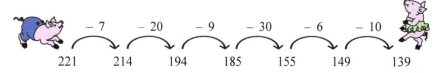

	221	214	194	185	155	149	139
		− 7	− 20	− 9	− 30	− 6	− 10

2.

a.	b.	c.	d.
9 × 2 = 18	3 × 10 = 30	7 × 2 = 14	5 × 10 = 50
7 × 10 = 70	6 × 2 = 12	12 × 10 = 120	4 × 2 = 8
11 × 2 = 22	9 × 10 = 90	3 × 2 = 6	11 × 10 = 110

3. a. half past 2   b. quarter till 7   c. 10 o'clock   d. quarter past 12

4. 6 × 3 + 8 = 26

Skills Review 40, p. 46

1. a. There are 12 more kilograms of bananas than strawberries.
   b. There are 48 kilograms of oranges and apples.

2. a. 120   b. 717   c. 0   d. 222

3. a. quarter till 3   b. 10 past 7   c. half past 12

4. a. 375 + 198 = 573; 573 − 375 = 198; 573 − 198 = 375
   b. 790 + 138 = 928; 928 − 790 = 138; 928 − 138 = 790

Skills Review 41, p. 47

1. a. odd   b. even 48   c. even 32

2.

a. 7 × 5 = 35	b. 4 × 5 = 20	c. 5 × 9 = 45	d. 4 × 4 = 16
10 × 5 = 50	4 × 12 = 48	2 × 5 = 10	11 × 4 = 44
3 × 5 = 15	4 × 3 = 12	5 × 12 = 60	9 × 4 = 36

3.

NOW:

- 5 minutes later 4:55
- 10 minutes later 5:00
- 20 minutes later 5:10
- 25 minutes later 5:15

4. Fifty-nine marbles are green.

5.

183	189	195	201	207
213	219	225	231	237

6. a. 254   b. 77   c. 527

Skills Review 42, p. 48

1. Blue arrows: $6 \times 4 = 24$; Pink arrows: $4 \times 6 = 24$

2. a. 4×9 is done first. $7 + 36 - 6 = 37$
   b. 5×6 and 7×2 are done first. $30 - 14 = 16$

3. a. 3:27   b. 11:39

4. a. $3 \times 3 + 5 \times 2 = 19$ eggs total
   b. $12 + 9 = 21$ guests were invited
   c. $7 \times 8 - 7 = 49$ apples are still in the bags.

Skills Review 43, p. 49

1. a. =   b. <   c. <   d. <

2. a. 23 minutes   b. 25 minutes   c. 44 minutes

3. a. Jade $59 +$ Gwen $81 = 140 -$ Roger $64 = 74$ points.
   b. Please check the student's answer. Answers will vary.

4.

a.	b.	c.	d.
$9 \times 11 = 99$	$2 \times 3 = 6$	$11 \times 11 = 121$	$4 \times 3 = 12$
$7 \times 11 = 77$	$6 \times 3 = 18$	$12 \times 11 = 132$	$12 \times 3 = 36$
$10 \times 11 = 110$	$10 \times 3 = 30$	$4 \times 11 = 44$	$5 \times 3 = 15$

Chapter 5: Money

Skills Review 44, p. 50

1.
   a. Rocket is seventh in line.
   b. Hamster is second in line.

2. a. $12 \times 9 = 108$; $4 + 6 = 10$ b. $180 - 30 = 150$; 70

3. She started at 2:50.

4. a. 456   b. 701   c. 162   d. 844

5. $5 + 21 = 26$

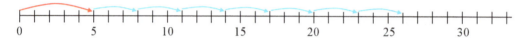

Skills Review 45, p. 51

1. a. 1:35; 1:45   b. 10:20; 10:30

2.

a. Add 40.	b. Add 15.
219	65
259	80
299	95
339	110
379	125
419	140

3. a. 530   b. 990   c. 60   d. 610

4. She went December 15th.

5. Seven plus twelve equals nineteen days.

6. Alex has more oranges. He has one more orange than Conrad has.

7. a. $5 \times 6 = 30$	b. $9 \times 9 = 81$	c. $6 \times 3 = 18$	d. $3 \times 9 = 27$
$9 \times 6 = 54$	$9 \times 4 = 36$	$6 \times 7 = 42$	$8 \times 9 = 72$
$8 \times 6 = 48$	$9 \times 7 = 63$	$6 \times 10 = 60$	$5 \times 9 = 45$

Skills Review 46, p. 52

1. a. 98   b. 12

2. a. 66¢   b. 95¢   c. 72¢

3. Jason worked ten and a half hours.

4. Veggie Village had 236 inhabitants originally.

5. $3 \times 4 - 0 \times 7 = 12$ legs more.

Puzzle corner:

$5 \times 9 - 8 = 37$ $72 - 4 \times 12 = 24$ $9 \times 4 + 4 \times 7 = 64$

$17 + 6 \times 8 = 65$ $43 - 8 - 6 = 29$ $(13 - 6) \times 3 + 5 = 26$

Skills Review 47, p. 53

1. a. 10:45   b. 7:30   c. 3:15   d. 8:45

2.

a.	b.	c.	d.
$2 \times 12 = 24$	$4 \times 7 = 28$	$7 \times 12 = 84$	$8 \times 7 = 56$
$6 \times 12 = 72$	$11 \times 7 = 77$	$12 \times 12 = 144$	$12 \times 7 = 84$
$9 \times 12 = 108$	$5 \times 7 = 35$	$4 \times 12 = 48$	$3 \times 7 = 21$

3. $23 + ? = 60$; $60 - ? = 23$ $? = 37$

4. a. 25   b. 38   c. 225

5. a. $6.35   b. $2.17

Skills Review 48, p. 54

1. a. Change: $8.50   b. Change: $1.55   c. Change: $7.75

2. a. He saw 28 more birds.   b. Wednesday and Thursday total 42 birds.

3. a. $4 \times 9 = 36$ and $6 \times 7 = 42$ Farmer Smith has more cows. He has 6 more cows than Farmer Jacobson.
   b. She has 7 bags. $84 - (12 + 12) = 60$ good rolls left.
   c. $6 \times 4 + 17 = 41$ He harvested 41 watermelons.

Chapter 6: Place Value with Thousands

Skills Review 49, p. 55

1. a. half past nine   b. a quarter past eleven   c. twenty-five minutes till eight   d. a quarter till three

2.

a.	b.	c.	d.
$2 \times 8 = 16$	$5 \times 8 = 40$	$1 \times 8 = 8$	$4 \times 8 = 32$
$7 \times 8 = 56$	$3 \times 8 = 24$	$6 \times 8 = 48$	$9 \times 8 = 72$
$10 \times 8 = 80$	$12 \times 8 = 96$	$8 \times 8 = 64$	$11 \times 8 = 88$

3. Please check the student's answer. Answers will vary.

4. a. $9.65   b. $7.15   c. $6.80

Skills Review 50, p. 56

1. a. $23.17   b. $72.97

2. a. 0   b. 30   c. 264   d. 24

3.

XXVIIII = light blue
CCLXXVII = purple
XLI = brown
CCXCVII = pink
LXXXVIII = yellow
CCLXVIIII = dark green
XXXII = red
CCCLXXXI = light green
CXLVI = gray
LXXVIII = dark blue
LIIII = orange
CXXIII = yellow

4. a. $14 < 15$ b. $24 = 24$ c. $40 > 35$
   d. $40 < 42$ e. $70 < 77$ f. $72 < 108$

5.

from	5:15	12:07	7:41	2:24	10:38
to	5:43	12:22	7:55	2:39	10:56
minutes	28	15	14	15	18

Skills Review 51, p. 57

1.

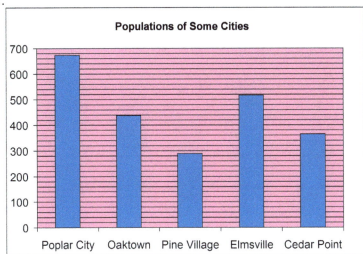

2.

a. Six thousand two hundred five	thou-sands	hund-reds	tens	ones
	6	2	0	5

b. Two thousand sixty-three	thou-sands	hund-reds	tens	ones
	2	0	6	3

3. $30 – $17.50 – $5.75 = $6.75 Shirley's change was $6.75.

4.	a. 3:33	b. 6:17	c. 9:51	d. 11:09
25 min. later	3:58	6:42	10:16	11:34

Skills Review 52, p. 58

1.

a.	b.	c.	d.
$6 \times 8 = 48$	$9 \times 5 = 45$	$2 \times 6 = 12$	$3 \times 11 = 33$
$3 \times 2 = 6$	$4 \times 12 = 48$	$10 \times 8 = 80$	$7 \times 4 = 28$
$8 \times 12 = 96$	$11 \times 7 = 77$	$1 \times 9 = 9$	$5 \times 10 = 50$

2. She needs to start cleaning her room at 2:35 or 25 minutes till 3.

3. a. 12th   twelfth   b. 42nd   forty-second
   c. 81st   eighty-first   d. 93rd   ninety-third

4. Please check the student's answer. Answers will vary.
   343 + 57 = 400

5. a. 4,078   b. 9,150

Mystery number: 21.
Sixty-three is also a correct answer, if we consider the phrase "in the table of 3" to mean "a multiple of 3", and similarly, "in the table of 6" to mean "a multiple of 6", but 3rd grade children are not likely to know that yet. Therefore, students are not required to give 63 as a solution, but some may find it.

Skills Review 53, p. 59

1. 169 + 181 + 121 = 471 miles.

2. 2 × 195 − 2 × 167 = 56 miles further

3. a. 677 < 767   b. 1,100 = 1,100   c. 2050 < 5,200

4. a. 3:55   b. 12:20

5. bicycle about $260 + helmet about $60 = about $320

6.

587	581	575	569	563
557	551	545	539	533

Skills Review 54, p. 60

1. a. ? − $5215 = $2830; ? = $8,045 originally.
   b. 1250 − ? = 830; ? = 420 hens did not lay an egg that day.

2. a. 25 − 9 + 8 = 24   b. 9 + 84 = 93

3.

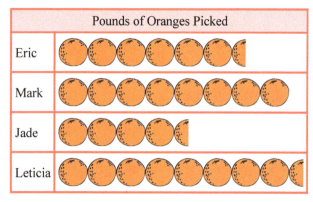

4. a. 5 hours   b. 14 hours

5. a. 6 half dollars   b. 9 half dollars   c. 5 half dollars and 1 quarter

Skills Review 55, p. 61

1. a. I have $12.59 originally. I will have $8.64 left after buying the shampoo.
   b. I will have $3.09 left after buying the gloves.

2. $1,285 - (625 + 248) = 412$

3.

	a.			b	
1	12		5	45	
2	24		6	54	
3	36		7	63	
4	48		8	72	
5	60		9	81	
6	72		10	90	
7	84		11	99	
8	96		12	108	

4. $30 - 12 + 28 = 46$ days till their anniversary.

5. a. a quarter past 1   b. half past 4   c. a quarter till 10   d. 12 o'clock

Skills Review 56, p. 62

1. a. 8,243   b. 8,533   c. 8,940

2. a. $1.35 change; can be a one-dollar bill, 1 quarter, 1 dime and 1 nickel.
   or 5 quarters, 1 dime and 1 nickel, or 1 dollar, 3 dimes and 1 nickel,
   or 27 nickels, or 13 dimes and 1 nickel, or 4 quarters, 6 nickels and 5 pennies, etc.

   b. $5.52 change; can be a five-dollar bill, 2 quarters and 2 pennies, or 22 quarters and 2 pennies,
   or 5 one-dollar bills, 5 dimes and 2 pennies, etc

3. a. $49 - 9 = 40 = 5 \times 8$ She had six cakes.
   b. $5 \times 11 + 8 \times 3 + 10 \times 4 = 119$ plants.
   c. $119 - 3 \times 9 = 92$ plants left.

Chapter 7: Geometry

Skills Review 57, p. 63

1.

a.	b.	c.	d.
$3 \times 7 = 21$	$9 \times 2 = 18$	$1 \times 10 = 10$	$8 \times 4 = 32$
$5 \times 12 = 60$	$2 \times 11 = 22$	$7 \times 6 = 42$	$9 \times 11 = 99$
$12 \times 3 = 36$	$5 \times 8 = 40$	$10 \times 5 = 50$	$8 \times 8 = 64$

2. a. 1,211; $1211 + 4819 = 6,030$ b. 3,678; $3678 + 5723 = 9,401$

3. Megan 24 minutes and Gary 26 minutes. Gary took 2 minutes longer to eat lunch.

4. a. Change $3.15   b. Change $6.40

Puzzle corner:

$9 \times 7 - 5 = 58$ $16 - 2 \times 6 = 4$ $7 \times 8 - 4 \times 9 = 20$

Skills Review 58, p. 64

1. 4600 4700 4800 4900 5000 5100

2. a. a quarter till 2   b. 20 past 5   c. a quarter past 11

3. $6 \times 8 + 9 - 34 = 23$ pieces of cake left.

4. $36.44 - (\$15.95 + \$7.99) = \$12.50$ for the unmarked shirt.

5. a. 600   b. 7,200   c. 4,800

6. a. <   b. >   c. >   d. <

7. a. 8,400   b. 2, 600   c. 6,800

Skills Review 59, p. 65

1. $3700 + $400 = $4,100; exact: $4,122

2. a. about 600 plus about 700 = 1,300 pounds total
   b. about 200 fewer pounds

3. a. 600   b. 7,200

4. Please check the student's work. Answers will vary. For example:

5. a. $25 - (9 \times 2) = 7$ b. $(6 + 5) \times (4 - 4) = 0$ c. $6 \times 3 + (2 \times 2 - 4) = 18$

Skills Review 60, p. 66

1. a. 0   b. 593   c. 32   d. 66

2. 7 × 12 + 9 × 10 + 7 = 181 flowers originally

3. a. 3:34   b. 9:49   c. 1:14   d. 11:19

4. Please check the student's answer. Answers will vary.

5.

1220	1210	1200	1190	1180
1170	1160	1150	1140	1130

Skills Review 61, p. 67

1.

a.	b.	c.	d.
4 × 7 = 28	1 × 6 = 6	4 × 4 = 16	8 × 4 = 32
9 × 11 = 99	5 × 9 = 45	12 × 2 = 24	8 × 8 = 64
5 × 3 = 15	12 × 12 = 144	9 × 6 = 54	10 × 6 = 60

2. a. 36 inches   b. 44 cm

3. a. She has $156.37 left.   b. Her change was $8.05

4.

7 8 1 2	2 4 8 3	8 2 3 6	9 0 4 7
− 4 5 5 8	+ 1 1 7 9	− 6 2 7 6	+ 3 6 0 2
3 2 5 4	1 3 0 4	1 9 6 0	5 4 4 5

Skills Review 62, p. 68

1. a. 91¢   b. 57¢

2. a. CCCXCIV   b. CCLVII   c. CCXIV   d. CIX

3. 3,045 − 1,438 − 672 = 935

4. 6:35   6:15

5. 8 + 8 + ? + ? = 40; ? = 12 cm

Skills Review 63, p. 69

1. a. They sold 55 more hamburgers on Saturday.
   b. They sold 420 hamburgers.

2. 3 × 6 = 18; A = 18 sq units

3. a. a quarter till 8   b. 4 o'clock

4. a. 850 + 425 − ? = 825; ? = 450 points were lost
   b. ? − ($1,250 + $765) = $3,098; ? = $5,113 originally

Skills Review 64, p. 70

1. a. 2 × 2,878 = 5,756 miles
   b. 2 × 5834 – 2 × 3778 = 4,112 miles further

2.

a.	b.	c.	d.
3 × 6 = 18	12 × 11 = 132	8 × 10 = 80	7 × 9 = 63
7 × 12 = 84	9 × 9 = 81	7 × 2 = 14	12 × 5 = 60
6 × 7 = 42	9 × 3 = 27	5 × 8 = 40	6 × 4 = 24

3. a. 23   b. 19

4.

5 × (3 + 5)   =   5 × 3   +   5 × 5

area of the whole rectangle   area of the first part   area of the second part

Skills Review 65, p. 71

1. a. $12.48 – $9.95 = $2.53 left   b. $12.48 – $6.70 = $5.78 left

2. Check the student's answer. For example: Parts: 50 + 50 + 50 + 50 + 50 The total area is 250.

3. 7 × 9 – 6 = 57 pizzas were eaten.

Puzzle corner: 12 × 6 – 57 – 3 = 12 = ? × 6; ? = 2

Skills Review 66, p. 72

1. (5 + 9) × 7 = 98 sq ft

2. a. Mr. Elliot is 4th in line.   b. Mr. Craig is 13th in line.

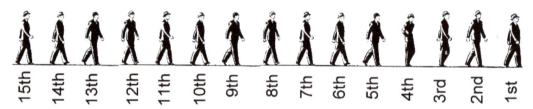

15th 14th 13th 12th 11th 10th 9th 8th 7th 6th 5th 4th 3rd 2nd 1st

3. a. September 5th   b. April 14   c. November 25th

4. a. 900   b. 8,400   c. 3,000

5. a. 27¢   b. 86¢   c. 262¢

Chapter 8: Measuring

Skills Review 67, p. 73

1. Estimate $3,700 + $200 = $3,900
   Exact: $3,732 + $238 = $3,970

2. a. Trains 1 and 3 have about 370 total passengers.
   b. 320 – 180 = 140 more passengers.

3. a. < b. > c. >

4. Please check the student's work. Answers will vary.

Skills Review 68, p. 74

1. a. 20 past 8 b. a quarter till 12 c. a quarter past 10 d. 10 till 2

2. 4 + 2 + 6 + 2 + 4 + 2 + 14 + 2 = 36 cm; P = 36 cm

3. a. 600 b. 2,300

4. a. triangle b. quadrilateral c. pentagon d. hexagon

5. 3,335

Skills Review 69, p. 75

1. a. 17 b. 27 c. 10 d. 17

2.

3. a. 4,673 b. 9,705

4. Check the student's answer.

5. a. 6 × 12 – 2 × 3 = 66 words left.
   b. $124 – $18 – 5 × $11 = $51 is what they still need.

Skills Review 70, p. 76

1. Please check the student's answers. Answers will vary.

2. Dylan had 21 not 20 shells. Brenna had 39 not 38 shells.

3.

tetrahedron

rectangular pyramid

square pyramid

4. a. 244	CCXLIV
b. 527	CCCCCXXVII
c. 392	CCCXCII
d. 184	CLXXXIV

5. Please check the student's answers. Answers will vary.

Skills Review 71, p. 77

1. $836 - 228 - 413 + ?$; $? = 195$

2. a. $7 \times 4 = 28$
$9 \times 9 = 81$
$2 \times 3 = 6$
$6 \times 5 = 30$
$11 \times 8 = 88$

   b. $12 \times 2 = 24$
$1 \times 0 = 0$
$9 \times 6 = 54$
$5 \times 12 = 60$
$7 \times 7 = 49$

3. a. 2 3/4 inches long
   b. There are 4 scraps of cloth that are at least 3 1/2 inches long.

4. a. $0.27   b. 582¢   c. $0.03

5. The other side is 18 feet.

Skills Review 72, p. 78

1. $4 \times (3 + 4) = 4 \times 3 + 4 \times 4$

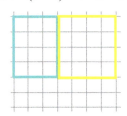

2. $1,330 - 80 + 50 = 1,300$ passengers

3. Justin's birthday is September 9th.

4. a. 4,600   b. 7,400   c. 2,600

5. a. inches   b. miles   c. feet   d. feet

Puzzle corner:

	8	3	7	2
−	5	2	9	3
	3	0	7	9

	3	8	6	9
+	1	3	3	9
	5	2	0	8

	9	9	0	7
−	7	1	0	9
	2	7	9	8

Skills Review 73, p. 79

1. a. 300   b. 700   c. 300

2. a. She arrived at 2:15.   b. She left at 4:45.

3. a. $50 − $35.80 = $14.20. The change could be one $10 bill, four $1 dollar bills and two dimes. There are other options.
   b. $20 − $16.48 = $3.52.   The change could be three $1 bills, two quarters and two pennies. There are other options.

4. a. $7 \times (15 - 9) + 8 = 50$ b. $(23 - 14) \times (6 + 3) = 81$

5. a. 10 inches   b. 1 1/2 inches

6. a. 374 cm   b. 809 cm   c. 694 cm

Skills Review 74, p. 80

1. a. Even 2 × 32   b. Even 2 × 49   c. Odd

2. Please check the student's work.

3. a. 16 lb   b. 7 oz   c. 1,000 lb

4. a. 7 × 5 + 4 × 12 − 8 = 75 razors.
   b. $65 − 6 × $9 = $11 extra she was given.
   c. 8 × (6 + 3) = 72 tomatoes.

Skills Review 75, p. 81

1.

NOW: • 5 minutes later 2:50   • 20 minutes later 3:05
        • 10 minutes later 2:55   • 25 minutes later 3:10

2. a. kg   b. kg   c. g

3. a. 9   b. 5   c. 9   d. 6

4. $15.63 total; $20 − ($12.35 + $3.28) = $4.37 change.

5. You can buy ten jars.

6. a. 140 cm^2 b. 132 ft^2

Chapter 9: Division

Skills Review 76, p. 82

1. a. quart   b. cup   c. pint

2. a. Estimate: 4,900 + 2,900 = 7,800; Exact: 7,794
   b. Estimate: 6,500 − 900 = 5,600; Exact: 5,563

3. a. $1.75   b. $0.29   c. $1.40

4. a. 57 inches   b. 150 inches   c. 96 inches

Skills Review 77, p. 83

1. a. 500   b. 3,200   c. 9,100

2. a. $57.30   b. $22.21   c. $69.33

3. a. $6 \times 6 = 36$ people   b. $24 \div 6 = 4$ teams

4. $3000 \div 300 = 10$ bottles

5. a. 5,000 ml   b. 2,600 ml   c. 7,040 ml

Skills Review 78, p. 84

1. 145 people dropped out of the race.

2. a. 1:37   b. 7:17   c. 5:47   d. 9:09

3. 3012 < 3048 < 3480 < 4138 < 4152 < 5028 < 5280

4. a. 4; 4   b. 8; $8 \times 7 = 56$ c. 7; $4 \times 7 = 28$

5. Please check the student's work. Answers will vary.

Skills Review 79, p. 85

1. a. 9 half dollars 1 quarter   b. 14 half dollars 1 quarter

2. a. Shane has saved about $400 more.   b. No, she needs about $300 more.

3. Answers may vary. Please check the student's work. Printed on a normal setting they should be:
   a. They are 9 cm 2 mm and 6 cm 4 mm.   b. 92 + 92 + 64 + 64 = 312 mm = 31 cm 2 mm perimeter.

4. a. $6 \times 9 = 54$; $54 \div 6 = 9$ b. $12 \times 4 = 48$; $48 \div 12 = 4$ cookies

Skills Review 80, p. 86

1. a. 96   b. 7   c. 6   d. 35

2. a. 11:30   b. 2:35   c. 12:45   d. 5:20

3. Please check the student's work. Answers will vary.

4.

a. 215 CCXV	b. 544 CCCCCXLIV	c. 371 CCCLXXI
216 CCXVI	545 CCCCCXLV	372 CCCLXXII
217 CCXVII	546 CCCCCXLVI	373 CCCLXXIII

Skills Review 81, p. 87

1. $2{,}348 + 3 \times 5 - 2 \times 4 = 2{,}355$ population now.

2. a. 10 hours 30 minutes   b. 13 hours

3. a. 9; $9 \times 12 = 108$ b. 7; $7 \times 7 = 49$

4. a. m   b. km   c. cm   d. m

5. a. He planted four rows.   b. He had 54 plants.   c. She had 72 pieces of pie.   d. She baked seven pies.

Skills Review 82, p. 88

1. a. impossible   b. 1   c. 9   d. 0

2. a. 132 lbs   b. 146 lbs

3. a. 35   b. 91

4. a. $2200 + 800 = 3{,}000$ b. $9600 + 400 = 10{,}000$

5. She made eight bouquets.

6. $(40 + 20) \times 6 = 380$ m^2

Skills Review 83, p. 89

1. a. 194   b. 626

2. They arrived July 28th.

3. a. 7,400   b. 9,400   c. 2,900

4.

a. $19 \div 6 = 3$ R1	b. $15 \div 8 = 1$ R7	c. $56 \div 6 = 9$ R2
$20 \div 6 = 3$ R2	$30 \div 8 = 3$ R6	$59 \div 6 = 9$ R5

5. $3000 \div 250 = 12$ glasses.

Puzzle corner: Twenty-four pints of water fit into a 3 gallon bucket.

Chapter 10: Fractions

Skills Review 84, p. 90

1. $28 ÷ 4 = 7$ cm

2. a. 320   b. 450   c. 280

3. A = 1,350

4. Her change was $8.37.

5. His change should have been $3.30 but they only gave him $3.20. They need to give him another dime.

6. a. 4 R3   b. 6 R6   c. 8 R2   d. 9 R2

Mystery number: 84

Skills Review 85, p. 91

1.

a. $\dfrac{5}{8}$ b. $\dfrac{8}{10}$ c. $\dfrac{2}{6}$ d. $\dfrac{1}{5}$ e. $\dfrac{3}{4}$ f. $\dfrac{6}{7}$

2. a. 900 grams   b. 1,600 grams

3. a. 88; $11 × 8 = 88$ b. 36; $6 × 6 = 36$ c. 8; $8 × 9 = 72$

4. $2 × (15 + 30) = 90$ feet perimeter.

5. $(28 + 42) ÷ 7 = 10$ packages of cookies.

Skills Review 86, p. 92

1. a. $12.95   b. $81.80   c. $31.30

2.

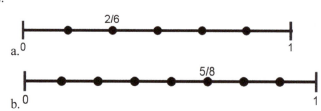

3. $4 × (8 + 6) = 4 × 8 + 4 × 6$

4. Please check the student's work. Answers will vary.

5. a. 6   b. 9   c. 10

Skills Review 87, p. 93

1. a. 2,185; 2185 + 1825 = 4,010   b. 2,263; 2263 + 4739 = 7,002

2.

18	12	15	13	20
27	36	25	29	23
69	72	75	66	71
142	137	144	135	148
279	288	263	287	251

3. a. 6   b. 0   c. 10   d. impossible

4. a. 8 pints   b. 2 cups   c. 16 cups

5.

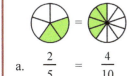 a. $3 \frac{2}{5}$  b. $5 \frac{6}{8}$

Skills Review 88, p. 94

1.

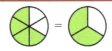

a. $\frac{2}{5} = \frac{4}{10}$ b. $\frac{1}{2} = \frac{6}{12}$ c. $\frac{4}{6} = \frac{2}{3}$ d. $\frac{6}{8} = \frac{3}{4}$

2. a. 5,300 > 3,500   b. 2,075 > 2,057

3. a. 4 × 6 ÷ 8 = 3 plums each.   b. 9 × $12 – $39 = $69   c. 8 × 2 + 5 × 4 + 29 = 65 stickers originally

4. 4000 – 9 × 300 = 1 liter 300 ml left.

Skills Review 89, p. 95

1. a. 4 R7   b. 23 R2   c. 9 R1   d. 6 R3

2. a. >   b. <   c. =   d. <

3. a. $8 × 9 = $72   b. $88 ÷ 8 = 11 hours   c. $36 ÷ 9 = 4 bags   d. $9 × 6 = $54

4. a. December 22nd   b. November 26th

5. a. 2 4/5 = 14/5   b. 2 9/12 = 33/12   c. 3 3/6 = 21/6

1. $6 \times 7 = 42$ $42 \div 6 = 7$

2. Estimate: $9300 - 5800 = 3{,}500$ Exact: $3{,}515$

3. a. 3:50   b. 6:30   c. 10:15

4. a.

   b. She would have to eat four pieces of cake.

Puzzle corner:

$62 - 9 \times 5 = 17$ $12 \times 4 + 9 = 57$ $7 + 8 + 6 \times 6 = 51$

CPSIA information can be obtained
at www.ICGtesting.com
Printed in the USA
LVHW05s1746100518
576645LV00001B/1/P